America Fever

Sven Skovmand

America Fever

The Dream of America

t Creative Education

The Dream of America

The series consists of

1 Europe and the Flight to America
2 America Fever
3 The Westward Journey
4 They Came to America
5 Gateway to America: New York City
6 Shattered Dreams: Joe Hill
7 Ireland in Flight

Editor (Danish edition): Flemming Lundahl
Picture Editor: Anita Amundsen
Covers: Nancy Arend
English Edition translated and edited by J. R. Christianson & Birgitte Christianson
Cover photo: USIS

Library of Congress Catalog Card No.: 81-71507
Author: Skovmand, Sven
      America fever.
Mankato, MN: Creative Education, Inc.
96 P.
8201   12591   811124
ISBN: 0-87191-706-8

Contents

emigrant = a person who leaves a country
immigrant = a person who comes into a country
migrant = a person who moves around within a country

The same person could be all three, leaving his or her native land first, then coming to America, and then moving from state to state inside America.

The Great Migration

52 Million People

Today, few Europeans emigrate to America. Few leave their native land. Europe has become rich and prosperous, offering just as many opportunities as other parts of the world.

That was not the case a hundred years ago. Thousands of families, millions of people traveled to America in those days: Norwegians, Danes, Swedes, Irishmen, Englishmen, Germans, Russians, Italians and many other nationalities. In the course of only seventy years, over 52 million people left their native countries to seek a new home on the other side of the Atlantic.

It was not a pleasant trip. During the early years, the ocean crossing took more than a month. That was when sailing ships were still being used. Later, ships powered by steam engines took over. Then the trip was faster. But it still lasted many days, and the emigrants had to put up with bad food and crowded living conditions. Few could afford a first class

Young Polish emigrant boards the ship to America in 1907

cabin. Most had to make the crossing in the crowded conditions of steerage, below the deck. For more information about travel across the Atlantic, see the volume, *The Westward Journey,* in this series on *The Dream of America.*

The journey was not over when the ship arrived in America. Another long and difficult trip remained before the final destination was reached. Immigrants had to travel on foot, by steamboat and horse drawn cart. They had to risk the possibilities of attack by Indians. They were often cheated by strangers as they passed through a strange new land, traveling among people whose language they could not understand and whose customs were new to them.

The trip to America meant saying goodbye forever to the old way of life, to home and to family—unless you could persuade your friends or relatives to come over and join you at a later date.

There must have been powerful reasons to make so many people strike out on a journey like that.

There was not much room in steerage. The poorest emigrants had to live here during the voyage across the ocean.

Fantastic America

Around 1850, only the eastern part of North America was settled by whites. The land west of the Mississippi was Indian territory. In the forests and the mountains, on the prairies and across the deserts, the Native Americans hunted and farmed, celebrated and waged war in their age old ways. Very few whites lived in the west at that

There were also dangers in America. Here, a gang of masked bandits attack a train.

time. Most of those who did were trappers who wanted to remain friends with the Indians.

The western part of America was as large as half of Europe, but there were less than a million Indians in the whole vast area. Well over 100 million people lived in the same amount of room in Europe.

Camp of Crow Indians in the 1830's.

Life in a Mandan Indian dwelling on the prairie. This tribe was later wiped out by smallpox.

Chief Crow Foot, 1885

The American Indians supported themselves by hunting, supplemented by a bit of farming, and that meant that they had to cover great distances following the game. A tribe of a few hundred people needed an immense area in order to find enough game. Therefore, the prairie seemed to be almost deserted. You could sometimes travel for days without seeing another human being.

White settlers saw the prairie as a great opportunity. To them, it was almost like something out of a fairy tale. For little or nothing, a person could settle down and acquire a farm. The land was fertile, and it was plentiful. There was almost always enough moisture in the form of rain and snow to water the crops.

The first farms of white settlers lay scattered on the great prairie. There was still plenty of game for the Indians. But more farmers arrived in time. Then there was less and less game. Irresponsible hunting by whites wiped out the buffalo. The Indians were left with no means of support. Those who survived were put on reservations.

The first whites on the prairie were trappers like this man from the middle of the nineteenth century.

When the railroad came to the prairie, buffalo still roamed in huge herds. Here they shoot streams of steam to get them off the tracks.

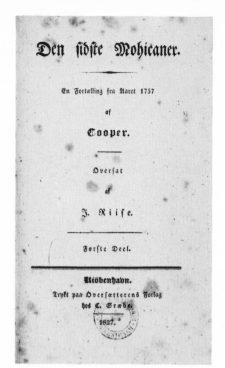

The Last of the Mohicans by James Fennimore Cooper was published in 1826. It became the first best seller about Indians. By 1827, this foreign language edition had appeared in Europe.

This whole process took less than thirty years in the whole great area of the plains.

There are many books about the battles between Indians and settlers. But in reality, the Indians were not defeated by bullets. They were defeated by plows, by fields of grain and by cows. Most of all they were defeated by the railroad.

What Did the Railroads Do?

Before the railroad was built, horse drawn wagons and ox carts were the only modes of transportation in many parts of America. They could travel where there were roads. West of the Appalachians, however, they ran into problems. Fallen trees and rushing rivers blocked the way. Further west on the open prairie, it was easy enough to find a trail, but they were dangerous because of bandits and Indians that lurked along them. Off the trails, you were completely on your own.

But there were still people who were willing to confront these problems. They kept moving further and further west, step by step.

Frontier life is described in the books by Laura Ingalls Wilder. In *Little House on the Prairie,* Laura and her family start out in a big covered wagon called a "prairie schooner." It was pulled by two horses. Rivers slowed them down. Sometimes they waited for days until a river went down and they could cross it. One time, Laura's father jumped into the river in order to get the horses to swim in the right direction with the wagon.

Later, it was easier to travel. In *By the Shores of Silver Lake,* Laura and her family take the train to their new home. In a few hours,

The Little House on the Prairie by Laura Ingalls Wilder has also been translated into many languages. This is a Danish edition.

they traveled a distance that would have taken them many days by covered wagon.

The American government encouraged the building of railroads. A law was passed in 1862 to insure that a railroad would be built across the whole continent from east to west.

12

Pioneers travel over the Oklahoma river in the 1880's.

Chuck Wagon.

The task was given to two railroad companies. One was to begin in Council Bluffs, Iowa. That city was already connected to the east coast by a railroad. The other company was to begin at Sacramento, California, and build eastwards.

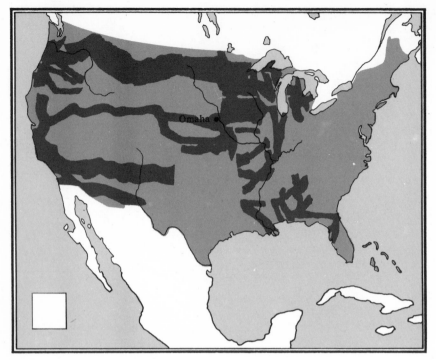

Land granted to railroads is marked in dark grey (exaggerated).

Above right. Work on the track. Many workers who built the western segment of the transcontinental railroad were Chinese. Many of those who built the eastern segment were Irish immigrants. These immigrants worked hard for low wages. American workers resented them, but they did a good job so they were hired.

Above far right. Locomotives from east and west meet in Utah, May 10, 1869. The rails were joined together with a golden spike, completing the first transcontinental railroad.

Below right. The interior of a passenger car around 1870. It was not fancy, but it was a big improvement over the prairie schooner.

Below far right. First class passenger car in 1900. By this time, the trains even had electric lights.

Below. Railroad bridges like this one had to be built to get trains through the mountains.

In order to get the companies interested, the government offered them alternate sections of public lands along the tracks to a depth of ten and even twenty miles. At the same time, the companies were promised large government loans for each mile of track they laid.

This got them going. The two railroad companies worked like mad to compete with each other and cover as much of the distance as they could. Despite difficult conditions and Indian attacks, the great distance was covered in only seven years. At one time, more than 20,000 men worked on the transcontinental railroad. During the last days before the line was completed, up to eight miles of track were laid each day.

16

The settlement of the prairie went into full swing after the Civil War. It was not just along the railroads that people settled. The government had passed the Homestead Act in 1862. It stated that anyone who settled on public land and cultivated it could have 160 acres free of charge.

The best interests of the Native Americans had not been considered in this law. Their situation soon became hopeless. The trickle of settlers turned into a stream and then into a great flood. New states on the prairies were filled with people in the course of a few years.

The last big confrontation between Indians and whites came in 1876. Led by Sitting Bull, the Sioux and their allies wiped out General Custer and all 264 of his men in the battle of the Little Big Horn. But the result of this Indian victory was that the government sent ever larger armies to crush the last hopes of Indian resistance. Within a few years, the plains Indians were defeated and living on reservations.

◄ Poster advertising the land rush to open Oklahoma to white settlement. Until 1889, the whole of Oklahoma territory had been a reservation settled only by Indians.

Pioneers wait for the signal to enter ► Oklahoma territory on April 22, 1889. At high noon, a shot was fired and they all raced off to claim free land. By nightfall, almost two million acres had been settled.

The Railroads and the Pioneers

Pioneers and railroads supported one another. The railroads made it easier for the pioneers to get to their land. It brought them supplies and allowed them to send their products to eastern markets.

In return, the pioneers provided an income for the railroads by purchasing tickets and sending freight. Prices sometimes seemed high, but the railroads could charge pretty much what they wanted. There was no competition from trucks or airplanes. The more settlers there were, the more the railroads earned.

The railroads put on campaigns to get more settlers into the new territories. They waged their campaigns in the older, settled parts of America along the eastern coast. They also advertised in Europe. The people of Europe listened eagerly to reports of the immense amounts of American land that lay idle and waiting to be taken and plowed.

America was empty of people compared to Europe. Europe was more overpopulated than at any other time in its history.

An early freight train with three locomotives. The tracks have just been laid and grass has not yet grown up along the grading.

Overpopulated Europe

"Peace, Potatoes and Vaccination"

Europe experienced a population explosion in the 1800's. In many ways, it was like the population explosion in the "third world" today. In some countries, the population doubled; in a few, it tripled. France was the only country in Europe where the population did not grow very much. The population of France remained more or less stable at around 25-30 million.

Why did the population of the rest of Europe grow so fast? The answer is not that the birth rate increased, but rather that the death rate went down while the birth rate remained stable.

A Swedish bishop, Esaias Tegner, put it like this, "The population is growing because of peace, potatoes, and vaccination." What did he mean by that?

Ever since the defeat of Napoleon at Waterloo in 1815, there had been peace in Europe. A few local revolts broke out in parts of the Russian, Austrian and Turkish empires. The Crimean War of 1853-56 was carefully contained so it did not become a major conflict. Two small wars were fought between Denmark and Germany, and Germany also fought

A miller and his family from Hillested in Denmark.

brief wars with Austria and with France. But compared to earlier centuries, this was not much. All in all, the nineteenth century was a time of peace in Europe.

This meant that young men were not killed on battlefields, crops were not destroyed and houses were not bombed out. This was Bishop Tegner's first point. The effects of peace, however, should not be overemphasized. Human societies are amazingly quick to overcome the disasters of war.

A bigger reason for the population explosion was that health conditions were improved.

Plague killed millions of people in the centuries from 1350-1650, but by around the year 1700, it seemed to have lost its effect. This was not because of any steps taken by medical authorities but was simply because the black rats that carried the plague were wiped out by brown rats. The brown rats did not carry the plague germs.

It was due to human efforts, however, that smallpox was defeated. Around the year 1800, an English doctor, Edward Jenner, discovered that milkmaids almost never got smallpox. He found out that this was because they had been infected with cowpox, a far less dangerous disease. This left them immune to smallpox. By giving

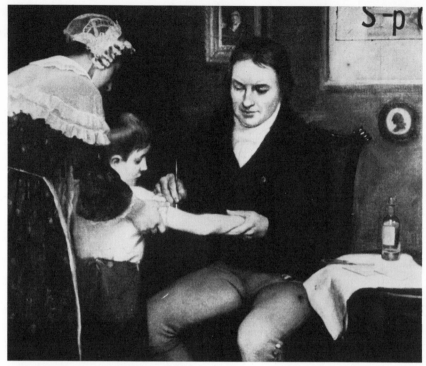

Dr. Jenner vaccinates a boy for smallpox.

Smallpox certificate from the year 1801.

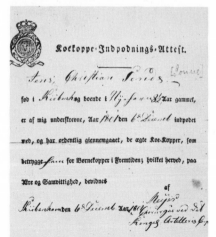

everybody cowpox, the spread of smallpox could be prevented. This was done by means of vaccination.

Vaccination was a great success. It is still the basis of the fight against smallpox. Many European countries had campaigns for vaccination around the year 1800. Results came quickly: the death rate fell.

Vaccination during a smallpox epidemic in Paris, 1867. The physician takes vaccine directly from a calf. There is no time to waste!

20

The importance of vaccination can be seen by comparing Sweden, where vaccinations were given to everyone, with Ireland, where very few vaccinations were given. From 1800-1850, only about 200 people died of smallpox in Sweden. But in the 1830's alone, about 5,000 people died *each year* of smallpox in Ireland.

The third and most important reason for the population explosion was that there was more food. In this, the potato played an important role.

The common white potato was simply unknown to Europeans until the middle of the eighteenth century. It came from the New World. It was first brought to Europe after Columbus' discovery of America. For more than two centuries, people could not bring themselves to eat these strange lumps from the earth.

There is a story about a learned man in France who went around offering free potatoes to anybody who would come and get them. Nobody came. Then he hit upon the idea of forbidding people to dig his potatoes. The next night his fields were pillaged. People dug them up to see what they could do with them.

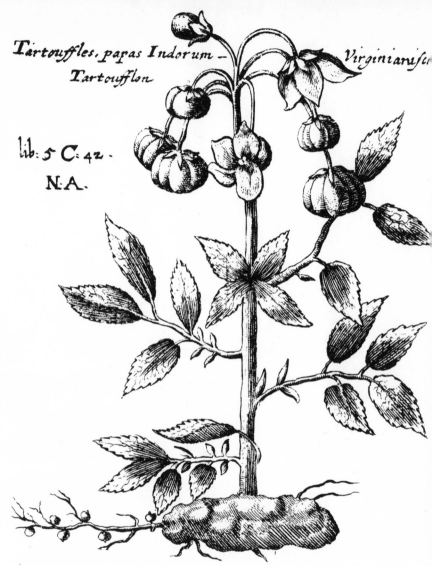

Drawing of a potato plant, 1695.

Once the potato had finally won acceptance, it became an important food crop. There were good reasons for this. Potatoes give a very large yield in comparison to other crops. Anybody with a vegetable garden knows that a small plot of potatoes will give

22

Digging, peeling and eating potatoes. Three drawings by Van Gogh, 1885.

24   Home distillation in Sweden, 1911. This was legal, but it used up grain and potatoes that could have been used for food.

enough for many meals.

In the 1800's, potatoes gave a yield that was four or five times better than wheat or rye. Potatoes could also grow in poor soil where these other crops could not. In Norway, they were even cultivated far north of the Arctic circle.

Potatoes made the farmers more prosperous. They could produce much more from the same amount of land. More often than before, poor people could eat their fill.

One of the "unnecessary" people, a 68-year-old man, outside his home.

"Unnecessary" People

The potato was a kind of insurance against famine for each family. Even in years of bad weather, they yielded a crop. When the small grain crops failed, there were always potatoes to fall back on. People no longer died of starvation when the crops failed as they had done in earlier centuries.

At the same time, the yield of small grain crops improved. New machines plowed and harvested. Farmers rotated crops and used fertilizer so the land stayed fertile from year to year.

Improvements in farming methods and the introduction of the potato were great steps forward. Together they meant that more food was available. The population grew. But this in turn led to new problems.

As the population increased, more people were living on the same amount of land. Some of them owned quite a lot of land, but others had to make do with less. Some lived in poor huts in the country and had no more land than a little garden plot.

These were the "unnecessary" people. Society did not need them, and they could not count on much help when they needed it.

The Danish historian, Peter Riismoller, has written a book about these people. Riismoller tells about people who lived under such difficult conditions that we can hardly believe it was true.

Daily Hunger

Sometimes people talk about the "good old days" when everything was cheap and taxes were low. But not many of us would care to trade places with the poor people of a century ago.

Every day was a fight for survival. Normal times were bad enough. When hard times came, the crop failed and there was no work, conditions became next to impossible.

Hunger came into their homes. Children died. Usually they did not actually starve to death. They died because they were too weak to resist diseases like the flu or even a bad cold.

25

Illustration from an 1884 edition of Dickens' novel about the poor house boy, Oliver Twist. Oliver asks for more soup, shocking the other children and the people in charge.

Where are My Two Boys?

Seven weeks ago, need and misery forced me to let my two boys, namely Peer, 11 years of age, and Ole, aged 7, wander around the parish of Gausdal seeking alms to keep themselves alive, since my husband and our eldest son have gone up north to seek work in order to earn something to maintain us through the winter.

But now that I, with much anxiety and distress, have searched in vain for seven weeks for my two boys, I have heard a report that they might have been seen in the Furunes area of Wang parish, but that the stray boys there are not able to say where their home is.

I call therefore upon every kind hearted person to whom these boys might come seeking alms, either to help bring them back to me, or else to send me information concerning their whereabouts, so that I can come and get them, and with thanks to God I will bless everyone who can give me any information concerning my children, who left home barefoot and very ragged.

Kirsti Hansdatter
living in Flinkslot cottage on the farm of Hole in Svadsum, Gausdal in Gudbrandsdalen.

Side 5. „Maa jeg faa lidt mere Suppe?"

Many authors of the nineteenth century described the hard life of poor people.

The English novelist, Charles Dickens, wrote about the orphan boy, Oliver Twist. He also wrote about a crippled boy, Tiny Tim. Hans Christian Andersen wrote the story about the little match girl who died on a cold city street.

Unhappy people like these, with little hope for the future, eventually became the emigrants who went to America. They did not mind if they had to live as servants or workers. All they knew was that they did not want to live the same difficult way as their parents. They wanted to find more hope for the future than Europe could offer them.

Frustrated Expectations

The Development of Industry

Europe in the 1800's was going through many kinds of dramatic changes all at once.

Machines had already been invented that made it possible for industry to expand. In 1703, an Englishman, Newcomen, had invented a steam engine that could pump water out of coal mines. It was a rather simple machine. It was operated by a child who sat and turned two faucets on and off. But this little machine meant that more coal could be mined.

Fifty years later, James Watt made a much better steam engine. His engine could be used to power factories and later, railroad trains and steamships.

The steam engine found widespread use in the textile industry. A number of machines had been invented to save labor. With these new spinning and weaving machines, one man could produce just as much thread and cloth as fifteen or twenty men could before.

Smoking chimneys and clattering machines soon told of the

The spinning jenny could spin up to one hundred times as many threads as an ordinary spinning wheel. It put many spinners out of work.

The McCormick reaper cut grain much faster than a man with a scythe.

progress that was being made. Textile factories came first to England, where the most important machines had been invented. The spread of factories was called the Industrial Revolution.

By the year 1800, the Industrial Revolution was in full swing in England. Other European countries followed right along. One factory after another shot up in areas where there was coal to fire the steam engines.

The prosperity of Europe grew. But not everybody shared in this prosperity. Many people found themselves worse off than ever before.

Farmers and Craftsmen

Vilhelm Moberg's novels of *The Immigrants* tell about a Swedish farmer, Karl Oskar Nilsson, who finally moved to America with his wife, Kristina. One bad year after another had made it impossible for him to pay the mortgage on his farm in Sweden.

The same thing happened to thousands of farmers throughout Europe. They had to sell their farms and try their luck somewhere else.

Drawing of a weaver's workshop by the Dutch artist, Van Gogh.

Times were especially hard for farmers in England. Estate owners bought up a lot of good farm land in the late 1700's. Many smaller farmers lost their land at that time. During the Napoleonic Wars, farmers large and small had been able to earn good money. No grain came into England from Europe because of the war, so prices went up to very high levels.

At the same time, the price of farm land went up. Farmers borrowed money to buy land. Peace came in the year 1815. The price of food went down instead of up, and farmers lost money. Many could not afford to pay back the money they had borrowed. They had to give up and sell their land.

The result was that soon hardly any English farmer owned the land he worked. Those who stayed in farming had to rent land from the big estate owners. Otherwise, they had to look for work in the cities and the factory towns. At the same time, new farming machinery and new farming methods meant that fewer people were needed to work on the land. So more and more had to head for the cities to look for work.

Many craftsmen also discovered that they were victims of the changing times. This was especially true of spinners and weavers. They were used to working at home and at their own pace. Now they had to

29

try to compete with the new machines, and of course that was impossible.

Competition with machines finally put them out of work. In 1805, a weaver in Manchester earned 25 shillings a week. As machine production increased, the weaver's wages fell. By 1818, his earnings had fallen to nine shillings a week, and by 1830, to six shillings a week.

Craftsmen really had no choice. They had to give in to industry. So they shut down their shops and looked for work in the factories. They got very low wages there, too—if they could get work at all.

In several places, people felt so helpless that they smashed the machines. Those who did this were called Luddites after the leader of the first group to do it, Ned Ludd. The police had to be called out against the Luddites. And it did not do any good to smash the machines. The use of machines kept increasing despite all opposition.

Machines took work away from people, but machines also created many jobs. Manufacturing by machine meant that more things could be produced and sold. All in all, machines created more jobs than there had ever been before.

But it took a long time before the effect could be felt. Jobs were not created fast enough to employ the rapidly growing population, including all those who had been forced to leave farming and craft production.

In 1897, about fifty years after the event, the German artist, Kathe Kollwitz, made a series of etchings of the weavers' strike of 1840.

Page 30 shows the protest march of the weavers.

The top picture on this page shows their unsuccessful attack on the factory.

The etching below shows a poor weaver's cottage where the family lives, works, eats and sleeps in one room.

Growing Unrest

Machines seemed to turn conditions topsy-turvy in nineteenth century Europe. Some people became very rich, especially manufacturers and estate owners who could take advantage of new methods and machines. Many, many more people became poor. Workers who were forced to move from the country to the city were, in many ways, worse off than before.

Drunk man leaving a bar. Drawing by the French artist, Daumier.

In the country, they had been part of the community. There had always been something to do or a little land to cultivate. In the city, they were just workers and that was all. There was nothing to fall back on if they were out of work.

Worst of all were the frustrated expectations. People who had moved from the country to the city had hoped for a better future. They did not find it. They saw great wealth in the cities, but it did not come their way. Some began to drink. Others became criminals. Dickens' novel, *Oliver Twist,* tells about them (see page 26). Others became so dissatisfied that they began to talk about a revolution. They wanted a violent change to tear down the old order and build up a more just society.

Some people sought the answer to their problems in religion. They sought to escape from their troubles and find a more perfect existence through faith.

The Religious Awakening

Among the emigrants in Moberg's novels are some like Kristina and Karl Oskar Nilsson, who emigrated for economic reasons. There were others like Kristina's rich uncle, Daniel, who did not have to leave because of economic necessity. His problem was that he had taken part in religious revival meetings and had preached the word of God without being ordained by the state church. That was against the law.

It seems strange to us that the authorities would interfere in people's religion. But the countries of

Adolph Tidemand's drawing of "The Fanatics," showing a religious sect meeting in a Norwegian farm house.

Europe did not have separation of church and state as we have in the United States. In most European countries, the church was part of the state. Defiance of the church was also defiance of the government. But in the nineteenth century, there were many common people who no longer believed what was preached by the state church.

One Danish lay preacher put it this way, "When the clergyman lacks faith, then the sheep dog goes in the shepherd's place." People took their religious life into their own hands.

The lay preacher defied the authorities of the state church. That got him into trouble with the government. Many of them were thrown in jail. No wonder they began to think about emigration.

Mormons

The authorities were not always the worst enemies of religious sects. Neighbors and villagers did not always like the work of the sects either.

This is illustrated by a former Mormon preacher who described how a sixteen year old boy was converted and what then happened to him.

"Henrik prepared to leave. He was met at the Mormon family's home by friendly Mormon elders.

Mormon preacher in Aalborg, Denmark. Photograph by Tonnies.

Hymns were sung about the beautiful valleys of Zion, and they were told of the wondrous works of the Lord which had been undertaken by the prophets and apostles. They told of the great temple of Zion, built on a hill, where they would soon gather and sit safely under the wings of the prophet, while the unrighteous heathens in Babylon would sigh and moan in pain and torment under the just punishments poured out upon them because they have rejected the wondrous light.

"At the same time, the man of the house and the man from the previous evening were down by the beach. They each had an ax along, and they chopped a big hole in the ice. It was February 4. The storm raged outside, it was very cold. The shore was lined with ice. When they came and said their job was done, Henrik shivered again. Everyone went down to the beach. Henrik took off his clothes on the ice, next to the gaping wet grave, and, shivering with cold, climbed in to his waist. The Mormon elder said the words used by the sect, and before he knew it, Henrik had been dunked under the water and was being helped out and into his clothes. He ran quickly up to the house. The cold water had warmed his young blood and in his inno-

Drawing of a Mormon baptism, 1853.

35

A Mormon confirmation, 1853.

cence, he believed it was the work of the Holy Spirit, given at his baptism.

"It was almost midnight. Henrik's parents, who thought this Mormon meeting was taking quite some time, sent after him and asked why he had been gone so long. Henrik, after receiving the 'holy baptism,' did not dare to lie any more. He admitted, to the astonishment of his parents, that he had been baptised down at the beach. His mother cried and said, 'Didn't I say when that man talked to Henrik that something bad was about to happen?'

"His father took a cane and gave him a good whipping. Henrik took it without complaining, because he had already been told that the holy would suffer persecution.

"After a week, however, the punishment was too much for Henrik. He traveled to Copenhagen with their permission, where a whole group of Mormons helped him get established. He soon got a job and used his free time to study Mormon writings. He was constantly asked to speak at Mormon prayer meetings, and in this way he got practice in giving Mormon sermons. About a year was spent in this manner. Henrik had shown an upright attitude and strong enthusiasm for the promotion of Mormonism. He was ordained into the ministry and sent out without money or baggage to preach Joseph Smith's gospel...

"A year later, Henrik was in the country north of Copenhagen. By this time, he had become an accomplished Mormon preacher.

Mormon missionary visits a village carpenter. Painting by Dalsgaard, 1856. The missionary is wearing blue jeans and cowboy boots.

Because he believed in his religion with his whole being, he always spoke with a captivating spirit that had an effect on his audiences. He won many friends. At the same time, he also made a vast number of enemies, because wherever he preached, there were stories of this or that person who had been converted by the Mormon, Henrik. He was persecuted everywhere.

"In one village where he organized a meeting, the teacher had all the school boys circle the farm he had entered. When the Mormons came out the gate, the boys were organized in regular battle formation with hands full of rocks. The stones rained down upon him, and he had to flee the town as quickly as possible.

"In another village where Henrik organized a meeting, windows were broken. The village ruffians sent him on his way with blows.

"The liveliest Mormon meeting was in Hollose on a Maundy Thursday. The people from all the villages around were invited to a meeting, and about three hundred had gathered. Words of abuse from the audience drowned out his sermon. His companion whispered that it would be best to leave. Henrik was pushed and shoved as he made his way through the crowd. When he finally got out-

side, he looked around for his companion, and saw him surrounded by a group of men.

"Henrik hardly had time to think before he found himself flat on his back from an unexpected blow. He got up and hurried down the road with the crowd right behind him. Their shouting and yelling increased. Henrik decided it was best to run. There was a pond in the middle of the village.

"'Throw the Mormon in the pond. Throw the Mormon in the pond,' they shouted. Henrik ran as fast as he could, full of fear. He got a few paces past the pond when a well aimed club hit him on the head and knocked him cold to the ground.

"When the young man came to, he was surrounded by a flock of Mormon sisters, who cried over him and helped him out of town. He looked awful when he was helped up from the dirt. His coat was covered with filth, and he had a big bump on his head. His companion arrived a half hour later. They had thrown him in the village pond, but otherwise he was all right."

Paradise on Earth

The real name of the Mormon church is the Church of Jesus Christ of Latter Day Saints. This church had been founded in

America in 1830 by Joseph Smith. He built up the religion on the basis of a book, said to have been written by a prophet named Mormon. It told the story of wandering Jewish tribes who became the original inhabitants of America.

The religious ideas of the Mormons sometimes seemed new and strange, but their way of life made a strong impression. Their society was exceptionally well organized. They had a strong sense of community. And they had both a prophet to lead them, and a paradise on earth in which to live.

The prophet after 1847 was Brigham Young. He took over the leadership of the church after Joseph Smith had been murdered while in prison in Illinois. The Mormon paradise was Utah. Today Utah is one of the fifty states, but at that time it was an isolated oasis on the edge of the Great Salt Lake, separated by great distances both from the eastern states and from California in the far west.

After the murder of their prophet, Joseph Smith, many of the Mormons left the eastern and midwestern states. They trekked across the country to the isolated valleys of Utah, determined to create a new home for themselves and determined to make the desert bloom. They were hard working and capable people, and they gradually did turn the desert into fertile land.

Mormon missionaries went out from Utah to other parts of the world. They tried to persuade converts to move to Utah and thereby strengthen the Mormon settlement as well as themselves.

In England and Scandinavia, the Mormon missionaries created a great deal of interest in their religion. They also aroused a great deal of opposition. Many people opposed the religious beliefs of the Mormons and their practice of adult baptism in "water holes and mud puddles." The rule that a man could have several wives as in the Old Testament also shocked many people.

The Mormons were persecuted, but this usually only strengthened their faith. Mormon converts knew the missionaries as friendly, capable, and often deeply religious people. They knew that much of what was said about them was lies.

They also knew that the Bible said the righteous would suffer for their faith.

About 30,000 Scandinavians travelled to America with the Mormons, in order to live in the Mormon Zion. Many others came from England and elsewhere. Their journey was much more carefully organized than that of most emigrants to America. Mormon ships and their whole system of travel arrangements were well known for their excellence.

The Mormon trek to the promised land of Zion in Utah.

Anti-Mormon propaganda like this tract
soon appeared in all the lands visited by the
Mormon missionaries.

Names of Mormon missionaries sent to the
Scandinavian countries in the years
1850-1864.

MISSIONÆRER UDSENDTE FRA ZION TIL SKANDINAVIEN.

Nr.	Navne.	Præste-dømme.	Bopæl i Zion.	Ankom til Kjöbenhavn.	Til'raadte Hjemrejsen fra Kjöbhn.	Arbejdstid.
1	Peter O. Hansen	Halvfjerds	Salt Lake City	11 Maj 1850	24 Nov. 1854	4½ Aar
2	Erastus Snow	Apostel	Salt Lake City	14 Juni "	4 Mar. 1852	1 A. 8 M.
3	John E. Forsgren	Halvfjerds	Salt Lake City	" " "	20 Dec. 1852	2½ Aar
4	Geo. P. Dykes	Höjpræst	Iowa	" " "	23 Juli 1852	Omt. 2 A.
5	Willard Snow	Höjpræst	Salt Lake City	26 April 1852	18 Aug. 1853	1 A. 4 M.
6	H. P. Olsen	Halvfjerds	Salt Lake City	4 Feb. 1853	26 Dec. 1853	Omt. 11 M.
7	E. G. M. Hogan	Höjpræst	Bountiful	12 " "	Nov. 1854	1 A. 10 M.
8	Knud Peterson	Halvfjerds	Lehi	" " "	29 Nov. 1855	2 A. 10 M.
9	John Van Cott	Halvfjerds	Salt Lake City	4 Sept. "	29 Jan. 1856	2 A. 4 M.
*	F. D. Richards	Apostel	Ogden	27 " 1854	5 Okt. 1854	8 Dage
*	Daniel Spencer	Höjpræst	Salt Lake City	9 Sept. 1855	11 Okt. 1855	1 M. 2 D.
*	Joseph A. Young	Halvfjerds	Salt Lake City	" " "	11 Okt. 1855	1 M. 2. D.
10	Hector C. Haight	Höjpræst	Farmington	" " "	4 Feb. 1858	2 A. 5 M.
*	Ezra T. Benson	Apostel	Salt Lake City	10 Sept. 1856	14 Okt. 1856	1 M. 4 D.
*	John Kay	Halvfjerds	Salt Lake City	" " "	14 Okt. 1856	1 M. 4 D.
11	Joseph W. Young	Halvfjerds	Salt Lake City	16 Aug. 1857	4 Feb. 1858	Omt. ½ A.
12	John Y. Greene	Halvfjerds	Salt Lake City	" " "	Dec. 1857	Omt. 4 M.
13	Iver N. Iversen	Halvfjerds	Pleas't Grove	" " "	20 Feb. 1858	Omt. ½ A.
*	Asa Calkin	Höjpræst	Salt Lake City	Okt. 1858	29 Okt. 1858	Faa Dage
*	Jabez Woodard	Höjpræst	Salt Lake City	20 April 1859	30 April 1859	10 Dage
(2)	John Van Cott	Halvfjerds	Salt Lake City	23 Nov. "	9 Maj 1862	2½ Aar
14	O. N. Liljenqvist	Halvfjerds	Goshen	" " "	21 April 1862	2 A. 5 M.
15	C. A. Madsen	Halvfjerds	Salt Lake City	3 Sept. 1860	15 April 1862	1 A. 7 M.
16	C. C. N. Dorius	Halvfjerds	Ephraim	" " "	30 April 1862	1 A. 8 M.
17	S. Christoffersen	Halvfjerds	Manti	" " "	18 April 1862	1 A. 7 M.
18	P. Beckström	Halvfjerds	Salt Lake City	" " "	April 1863	2 A. 7 M.
19	K. H. Bruun	Halvfjerds	Pleas't Grove	" " "	April 1863	2 A. 7 M.
20	H. P. Lund	Halvfjerds	Salt Lake City	" " "	30 April 1863	2 A. 8 M.
21	J. F. F. Dorius	Halvfjerds	Ephraim	" " "	30 April 1863	2 A. 8 M.
22	H. Olin Hansen	Halvfjerds	Hyrum	†4 "	9 Maj 1861	Omt. 8 M.
23	H. C. Hansen	Havlfjerds	Weber Co.	24 Sept. "	9 April 1862	Omt. 1½ A.
24	A. Christensen	Halvfjerds	Brigham City	" " "	April 1863	Omt. 2½ A.
*	A. M. Lyman	Apostel	Salt Lake City	10 Okt. "	4 Nov. 1860	Omt. 25 D.
*	C. C. Rich	Apostel	Salt Lake City	" " "	4 Nov. 1860	Omt. 25 D.
25	Jesse N. Smith	Höjpræst	Parowan	11 Jan. 1861	13 April 1864	3 A. 3 M.
26	W. W. Cluff	Halvfjerds	Provo	" " "	20 April 1863	2 A. 3 M.
27	J. P. R. Johansen	Halvfjerds	Provo	" " "	10 April 1864	2 A. 3 M.
*	(2)A. M. Lyman	Apostel	Salt Lake City	21 Aug. "	25 Okt. 1861	2 M. 4 D.
*	(2)C. C. Rich	Apostel	Salt Lake City	" " "	25 Okt. 1861	2 M. 4 D.
*	Geo. Q. Cannon	Apostel	Salt Lake City	†6 Sept. 1862	21 Sept. 1862	15 Dage
*	Joseph F. Smith	Halvfjerds	Salt Lake City	†" " "	21 Sept. 1862	15 Dage
*	S. H. B. Smith	Halvfjerds	Salt Lake City	†" " "	21 Sept. 1862	15 Dage
28	John Smith	Patriark	Salt Lake City	†" " "	13 April 1864	1 A. 7 M.
29	Hans C. Hansen	Halvfjerds	Manti	17 Sept. "	April 1863	Omt. 7 M.
30	A. W. Winberg	Halvfjerds	Salt Lake City	" " "	4 Maj 1865	2 A. 8 M.
31	Johan Svenson	Halvfjerds	Salt Lake City	" " "	4 Maj 1865	2 A. 8. M.
32	C. Holberg	Halvfjerds	Ogden	" " "	April 1864	1 A. 7 M.
*	C. W. West	Höjpræst	Ogden	Juli 1863	Juli 1863	Faa Dage
*	B. Young jun.	Höjpræst	Salt Lake City	" "	Juli 1863	Faa Dage
33	S. L. Sprague	Halvfjerds	Salt Lake City	8 Aug. "	‖25 Maj 1866	2 A. 9 M.
34	John Gray	Halvfjerds	Salt Lake City	" " "	Maj 1864	Omt. 9 M.
35	Geo. M. Brown	Halvfjerds	Provo	" " "	‖2 Juni 1866	2 A. 9 M.
36	John E. Evans	Ældste	Salt Lake City	" " "	April 1864	Omt. 9 M.
*	(2)Geo. Q. Cannon	Apostel	Salt Lake City	19 Aug. "	21 Sept. 1863	1 M. 2 D.
	John W. Young	Höjpræst	Salt Lake City	11 Maj 1864	24 Maj 1864	13 Dage

*Besögende. †Ankom til Kristiania. ‡Ankom til Korsöer. ⸰Fra Liverpool. Han arbejdede en
‖Fra Hamborg.   Del af Tiden i Tyskland.

Other religious sects were seldom so well organized in providing travel facilities to America. However, there were many others who emigrated for religious reasons. Persecuted religious groups naturally wanted to move to a place where they could join with people of the same belief and practice their faith in peace.

Of course it was not a new development for people to move to America for religious reasons. Some of the very first colonists were the Puritans who fled religious persecution in England. In later years, English Catholics and Quakers, French Protestants, German Lutherans and sectarians, and many others came to America to seek religious freedom, fleeing persecution in many parts of Europe.

Suppression of National Minorities

In 1864, Germany conquered the Danish province of Schleswig. The Danish speaking population came under German rule. Conditions were especially difficult for young men. They were subject to be drafted into the German army. Military service was for three years. What would these young men do if they were forced to fight on the wrong side in another war between Germany and Denmark?

Mormon family about to depart for America. Photograph by Tonnies.

Germans march into Paris in 1871. This German victory over France brought Alsace-Lorraine under German rule.

Map of Schleswig, 1862. Most of the population spoke Danish. Those in the southern part of the province spoke German, and those along the southwestern coast spoke Frisian.

In the first years after 1864, the Danes of Schleswig encouraged their young men to avoid military service at any cost, even by emigration. People had strong opinions on this matter. They spit at young men who chose to become German soldiers.

Later they changed their minds. If the Danes in Schleswig were to remain Danish, they realized that young men had to remain, even if it meant serving in the German army. This change of attitude slowed down the rate of emigration somewhat, but there was still a lot of emigration from the province. Within a period of about 50 years, 60,000 Danes out of a total population of only 160,000 left Schleswig. Very large numbers of them settled in the state of Iowa.

Many other places in Europe had the same kind of problems. Ethnic minorities lived under foreign rule. The French provinces of Alsace-Lorraine came under German rule when France lost the Franco-Prussian war of 1870-71. Czechs, Slovaks, Moravians, Croatians, Italians and Romanians were among the minorities ruled by the Austro-Hungarian Empire. Poland had been carved up by Germany, Austria and Russia so that no independent state of Poland existed (see map, page 53).

Coming under foreign rule was not new in Europe. The Danes themselves had ruled over all the Norwegians and a large number of Germans for centuries until the year 1814. The Swedish king ruled over Finns as well as Swedes for many centuries.

This had not caused the same kinds of problems in earlier generations because people had not considered language differences to be so important. They attached more importance to whether they shared the same religion, political allegiance, occupations, trade and family connections.

The Napoleonic Wars and nationalism changed this situation.

43

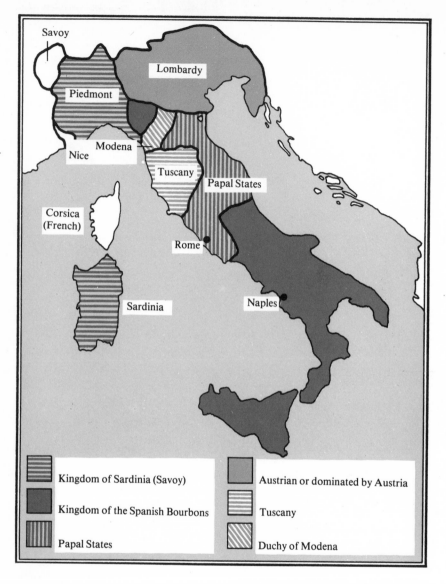

Savoy

Lombardy

Piedmont

Modena

Nice

Tuscany

Papal States

Corsica
(French)

Rome •

Sardinia

Naples •

	Kingdom of Sardinia (Savoy)
	Kingdom of the Spanish Bourbons
	Papal States

	Austrian or dominated by Austria
	Tuscany
	Duchy of Modena

Until 1861, Italy was divided into a number of states and territories. The kingdom of Sardinia-Savoy ruled over the island of Sardinia as well as Piedmont, Savoy and Nice. They later gave Savoy and Nice to France in return for help in the uniting of Italy. The Spanish Bourbons ruled the island of Sicily and the whole southern half of Italy. Austria ruled Lombardy and dominated all of northern Italy except Sardinia-Savoy. The Pope ruled the territory around Rome.

People at war discovered that they were different from those who spoke other languages. In every country, people became interested in the things that made them different from others—their language, customs and national culture. This interest was the beginning of nationalism. The national movement was a valuable movement in many ways.

When people of the same nationality began to talk about forming a country of their own, however, it could lead to serious problems.

For example, when a national movement started in Italy with the aim of uniting all Italians into one country, the Austrians became concerned. The northern part of Italy belonged to Austria at that time. If these Italians wanted to pull away from Austria to join a united Italy, then the other minorities ruled by Austria might get the same idea. Soon there would be nothing left of the Austro-Hungarian Empire.

Therefore, the rulers of Austria and other countries began to crack down on movements for national independence. In the year 1848, there were nationalist revolutions throughout Europe. They were all crushed. Many of the leaders emigrated to America. Others were

Political cartoon from 1867, showing the Prussian Iron Heels treading on a Dane in Schleswig.

Ei blot til Lyst.

En Slesviger, under det milde, preussiske Regimente.

thrown into prison.

But the Italians and other oppressed nationalities did not give up. Soon the only independent state in Italy, the kingdom of Sardinia-Savoy, began to support the cause of Italian national unity. A nationalist leader, Garibaldi, overthrew the Spanish Bourbon

Hungarian exile leader hailed in Philadelphia. From Illustrated London News, 1850.

rulers of southern Italy with an army of 1000 red-shirted nationalists. In 1861, Italy was united under the king of Sardinia-Savoy, who now became the king of Italy.

Nationalist revolutions in other lands were not always such a success as in Italy. A revolution in Poland in 1863, for example, was crushed by force by the Russians.

Hopelessness spread among many national minorities. Emigration to America seemed to be their only way out.

Where Did They Come From?

A Report from Ireland

"The Irish peasant is forced to starve, to beg, or to emigrate; he becomes in the eyes of those who rule him mere human garbage, to be shipped off and dumped anywhere."

The American writer, Henry George, wrote this in 1883 in his book, *Social Problems.* He went on to tell how big steamships on contract with the British government were calling "at small ports on the west coast of Ireland, filling up with men, women and children, whose passages are paid by their government, and then, ferrying them across the ocean...dumping them on the wharves of New York and Boston with a few dollars apiece in their pockets to begin life in the New World."

Ireland was not a poor country in Henry George's opinion. He told of a trip he had taken recently in Ireland:

"What surprises an American at first, even in Connaught, is the apparent sparseness of population, and he wonders if this can indeed be that overpopulated Ireland of which he has heard so much. There is plenty of good land, but on it are only fat beasts, and sheep so clean and white that you at first think that they must be washed and combed every morning. Once this soil was tilled and was populous, but now you will find only traces of ruined hamlets, and here and there the miserable hut of a herd. ...For the 'owners' of this land,

Irish fisherman's hut in Connemare. Illustrated London News, 1880.

who live in London and Paris, many of them never having seen their estates, find cattle more profitable than men, and so the men have been driven off. It is only when you reach the bog and the rocks, in the mountains and by the sea-shore, that you find a dense population. Here they are crowded together on land on which Nature never intended men to live. It is too poor for grazing, so the people who have been driven from the better land are allowed to live upon it—as long as they pay their rent...

"In spite of their painful industry the poverty of these people is appalling. In good times they just manage to keep above the starvation line. In bad times, when a blight strikes their potatoes, they must eat seaweed, or beg relief from the poor-rates, or from the charitable contributions of the world. When so rich as to have a few chickens or a pig, they no more think of eating them than Vanderbilt thinks of eating his $50,000 trotters. They are sold to help pay the rent. In the loughs you may see fat salmon swimming in from the sea; but, if every one of them were marked by nature with

Irish tenants being driven from their home. Illustrated London News, 1881.

the inscription, 'Lord So-and-So, London, with the compliments of God Almighty,' they could not be more out of the reach of these people....

"But the landlords—ah! the landlords!—they live differently. Every now and again in traveling through this country you come across some landlord's palatial home mansion, its magnificent grounds enclosed with high walls. Pass inside these walls and it is almost like entering another world—wide stretches of rich velvety lawn, beds of bright flowers, noble avenues of arching trees, and a spacious mansion rich with every appointment of luxury, with its great stables, kennels, and appurtenances of every kind. But though they may have these luxurious home places, the large landlords, with few exceptions, live in London or Paris, or pass part of the year in the great cities and the rest in Switzerland or Italy or along the shores of the Mediterranean..."

47

48   Conflict between Protestants and Catholics in Belfast, Northern Ireland. Illustrated London News, 1872.

The Tormented Land

Ireland was without doubt the country in Europe that sent the most people to America in comparison to its size. More than four million Irish emigrated to America, and this was from an island smaller than the state of Maine. There were good reasons for the great emigration from this small island.

Ireland came under English rule in the 1170's. Over the centuries, a large amount of land had come into English ownership. Monasteries had once owned a lot of land in Ireland, but these monasteries were dissolved in the 1500's and their land was also given to rich Englishmen.

During Cromwell's time around 1650, Irish conditions went from bad to worse. A big Irish revolt was crushed, and the English did everything they could to break the pride of the Irish. The fact that the Irish were Catholics, whereas the English were Protestants, added religious hostility to an already strained situation.

The Irish were pushed out of the northeastern part of their own country—the present area of Ulster or Northern Ireland. A new population of Scottish Protestants was brought into that part of Ireland by the English. Throughout the whole island, English landowners kept expanding their holdings until they owned over three-fourths of the countryside. Only the worst land was left for Ireland's own people.

The potato was introduced to Ireland in the 1740's and quickly became a widespread food crop. Ireland's mild climate was good for growing potatoes. Before long, most of the Irish people were living on potatoes and milk. They also grew grain, but they did not use it themselves. They sold it to pay their rent to the landlord.

Potatoes and milk does not sound very appetizing as a steady diet, but it could keep you alive. This diet more or less gave the required nourishment. Therefore, the population grew in numbers despite the fact that some of them were constantly emigrating, especially to England.

By the 1840's eight to nine million people lived in Ireland. That was more people than in all of North America west of the Appalachian mountains. Almost all of the Irish were farmers. There was little industry. People with money preferred to invest it in England, where the possibilities for selling goods were greater.

The catastrophe struck Ireland in 1845. Potatoes were hit by a

disease that made them rot soon after they were dug out of the ground. This was the much feared potato blight. The volume, *Ireland in Flight,* in this series, *The Dream of America,* tells more about this problem. The potato blight spread all over Europe, but the effects were worst of all in Ireland. Between one and two million people died of starvation and disease.

Many Irish chose to flee—either across the Irish Sea to England, or else over the Atlantic to America. Even the voyage to America was quite inexpensive. Many Irish

49

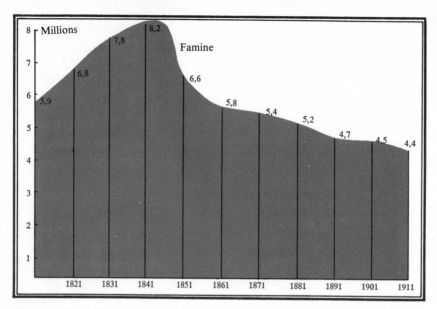

The population of Ireland 1810-1911.

estate owners or county authorities paid at least a part of the cost of passage. If a person could raise a small amount for himself, the authorities were frequently willing to provide the rest.

The Irish traveled to America under terrible conditions. The emigrant ships were called "floating coffins," and many died during the ocean crossing. In the New World, it took a long time for them to find tolerable living conditions. But at least they had a chance to survive. That mere chance encouraged other Irish to follow.

Today there are only four and a half million people in Ireland, half as many as when the potato famine began. Large numbers of Irish still emigrate. Thirty thousand leave every year, but now the main destination is England.

Departure. Illustrated London News, 1881. ▶

Russian Jews

The Irish were not the only people who came to America to save their lives. East European Jews, especially Russian Jews, did the same thing at a later time.

The Jews had a long history of persecution. In the first centuries after the time of Christ, they were driven out of Palestine by the Romans. Groups of Jews settled in widely scattered locations around the shores of the Mediterranean and Black Seas. Some of them became farmers. Others became traders and money lenders.

The Roman Empire was falling apart. In those days, people lived together as tribes. The Jews lived as separate tribes among other peoples. They kept their own religion and customs. Christianity began to spread among the pagan tribes, but the Jews did not become Christians. By around the year 800, they found themselves living among people who were almost all Christians. The Jews still kept their own religion and ways.

People started to be suspicious of them because they were different. Christians of the Middle Ages knew that Christ had been killed by Jews. Sometimes they blamed the Jews who were still living among them as a separate people. Angry mobs attacked the

52

Buying an apple from a Jewish vendor in Eastern Europe.

Jewish school in Eastern Europe.

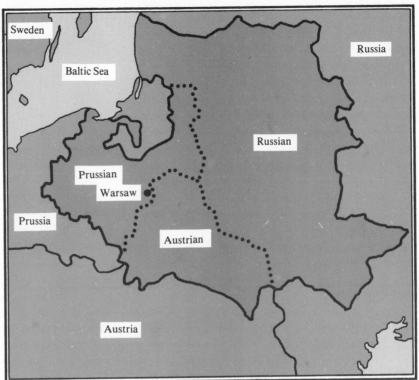
How Poland was partitioned between Prussia, Russia and Austria.

Jewish milkman in Eastern Europe.

homes of Jews. They were lucky if they escaped alive.

The age of the Crusades, from around 1100 to 1300, was a bad time for the Jews. For over 400 years, Christian communities had been under attack from the Moslems. Many of them had been completely destroyed. Now the Christians counterattacked. In their religious excitement to fight for their faith, many of them also attacked Jewish communities within Christian countries.

Around the year 1350, a great catastrophe struck western Europe. It was a plague called the Black Death. In some areas, as many as one out of every three people died. This was one of the worst plagues the world has ever seen. Nobody knew what to do. Some blamed it on the Jews. They attacked Jewish communities. They drove the Jews out of France, England and parts of Germany. Many Jews were killed. Those who survived fled eastwards. They finally came to

53

the great kingdom of Poland. Here they could live in peace. They settled down.

For 500 years, a large percentage of the world's Jews lived in Poland. At that time, Poland ruled an empire much larger than the present country of Poland. But it was not a strong empire, and it grew weaker as time passed. In the years 1772-1795, it was simply divided up and taken over by the strong neighboring kingdoms of Prussia, Austria and Russia. Most of the Jews lived in the large part of Poland that now came under Russian control.

The Jews had established a good life for themselves in Poland. They had taken over much of the trade and craftsmanship in the country. Many were farmers or fishermen. Some had become overseers and managers on large estates. In this way, they could become prosperous.

But overseers were not very popular with the Polish, White Russian and Ukrainian peasants who had to work under them. If the peasants did not like their Jewish overseer, they might end up becoming hostile to all Jews. Then if the ruler did not protect the Jews, there could be trouble.

This happened in the parts of Poland taken over by Russia. Con-

Photograph of a wandering Jewish craftsman in Russian Lithuania.

A Jew attacked by a mob in Kiev, Russia. Soldiers look on but do nothing. Illustrated London News, 1881.

ditions for Jews started to become worse. They could only live in certain areas. Their educational opportunities were cut back. At the same time, the position of the Tsar of Russia became weaker because of growing opposition to his rule. He could not protect the Jews. On the contrary, the Tsar began to blame the Jews for everything that went wrong.

This happened on a large scale when Tsar Alexander II was murdered in 1881. The murderers were young revolutionaries who wanted to destroy the Russian Empire. Among them was a young Jewish woman. This led the new Tsar and his advisors to start a number of pogroms—the much feared persecutions of the Jews.

"There is only one way to solve the Jewish problem," said a leading advisor to the Tsar. "One third of the Jews must die, one third must emigrate, and one third must become Russians."

55

A Jewish emigrant living in America visits his parents in Eastern Europe.

Right: Left behind. A Jewish woman with her grandchild whose father has emigrated to America.

Far right: Seven-year-old Jewish boy from Poland, on his way to America alone.

56

This terrible threat did drive thousands upon thousands of Jews to flee. This time they fled westwards. Most of them came to America, though some also settled in the western European countries. By around the year 1900, more than one million Jews had left Russia.

Later the number was more than doubled. In 1905, Russia lost a war with Japan. Following this defeat, a big revolt broke out in the Russian capital of St. Petersburg (now Leningrad). It was crushed.

New persecutions of Jews soon followed. Their homes and shops were attacked and plundered. Those Jews who could escape set off on the long journey to America.

Today the USA has more Jews than any other country in the world. In New York City alone, there are as many Jews as in the whole state of Israel.

More information about Jews can be found in the volume, *Europe and the Flight to America,* in this series on *The Dream of America.*

Immigrant Origins

Where else did the immigrants come from?

This question can be answered in two ways. The first is to list the countries that sent the largest total

Above: Jewish boy in America receives religious instruction from his grandfather while his grandmother listens.

Right: Italian poverty. Woman in Sardinia spins wool outside her home.

numbers of immigrants. They are all big countries: England, Germany, Austria-Hungary, Italy and Russia (including Russian and Polish Jews).

But a whole new list appears if we figure the emigrants as a percentage of the total population in the country. Ireland is number one and Norway is second. England and Sweden share the

57

557b
Eieret Wilse

Emigrantreisens begyndelse.

third spot. Further down the list comes Denmark and Germany. Far down on the list come Austria-Hungary, Russia and Italy. Emigration began later in these countries, and it never affected as large a percentage of the population.

The great wave of immigration lasted until 1914. Then World War I broke out and put an end to immigration. After the war, the USA set up quotas to limit immigration.

Emigration began earliest in those countries that were closest to America. They were the ones on the Atlantic coast of Europe. First came England and Ireland, then Germany and the Scandinavian countries. Finally, Eastern Europe and Italy joined in.

Norway was a very mountainous country. The people were poor, and the population was growing rapidly. This made many of them even poorer because it meant that there were more mouths to feed. The Norwegians lived by the ocean, and they already had many ships. They were a seafaring people. So they started to emigrate at an early date and kept on emigrating right up to 1914.

Norwegian emigrants beginning their long journey to America.

Why Not France?

It seems strange that France played such a small role in emigration. France was a large country with a population of 25 million. But only about half a million Frenchmen emigrated.

The reason is simply because the French were better off than other people in Europe. Therefore, they did not have the same desire or need to emigrate.

French soil was rich, and it was much better distributed than in England and other countries. French peasants had a fairly high standard of living. They also had smaller families than in other countries, so the land did not need to be divided into smaller plots.

The population of France grew very little, and industry could employ most of those who moved to the cities.

Of course there were also social problems in France. Those problems were the background for the French revolutions of 1789, 1830, 1848 and 1871. However, many of the problems were solved following these revolutions.

Because France did not have the population pressures of other countries, Frenchmen had a better chance to build a satisfactory future in their own land.

Immigrant Fates and Fortunes

The tall man in the picture above is Carlo Tresca, an Italian American labor leader of the Industrial Workers of the World (I.W.W.). He is standing with three immigrant workers.

The picture on the left shows Sointula ("place of harmony"), a utopian colony organized in 1903 by Finnish immigrant workers on Malcolm Island, B.C., Canada. These former railway workers and coal miners formed a colony in the wilderness where they could escape from a bleak existence and live in peace and cooperation.

Rock Springs Wyo. July 4, 1917

The picture above shows Yugoslavians, many of them miners, in Rock Springs, Wyoming. The picture was taken during World War I. They are showing their loyalty to the American flag. At the same time, they are urging America to help their native country gain its freedom from foreign rule.

The pictures on this page show Eduardo Migliaccio (1882-1946), known professionally as "Farfariello." He was a famous character actor in the Italian American theater. Here he is shown in three of his roles. In the lower left, he is dressed as a World War I soldier and holds the American and Italian flags. Italy and the USA were allies in World War I.

Scandinavian Emigration

About 300,000 people came to America from Denmark. At that time, Denmark had a total population of only around two million people. This means that 15 out of every 100 Danes left the country.

The Danish rate of emigration was high, but not in comparison to the very high rates of emigration from the other Scandinavian countries of Sweden and Norway.

Between 1850 and 1914, one million Swedes and 750,000 Norwegians left their native countries to come to America. In terms of percentages of the total population, the figures for Norway are especially high. Less than two million people lived in Norway at that time.

In many ways, the three Scandinavian countries are very much alike. They all speak related languages. They share the same Lutheran religion and much of the same history. Why were there such great differences in the numbers of people who emigrated from the various countries? Were conditions so much better in Denmark than in Norway and Sweden?

There were some differences. The soil was better in Denmark, and it was distributed more fairly. The population was growing more slowly in Denmark than in Nor-way. Part of this growing Danish population was absorbed by colonizing new land in the heath districts of the country.

Up to around 1850, many Norwegians left their homes in the southern part of the country and went off to colonize the far north of Norway. Wheat, rye and barley would not grow there, but potatoes would, and the sea was rich in fish. But after 1850, there was no more room for settlers in northern Norway. All arable land was now taken up, and the same was true throughout the whole country. Towns were few and far between in Norway. People who did not own land had a choice of living as poor cottage dwellers along a country lane or emigrating to America. Vast numbers chose to emigrate.

In some parts of Sweden, the custom was to divide a farm among all the heirs. Soon the farms were so small that many farmers sold them and emigrated to America. In other parts of Sweden, the farms were large but only a few people owned them. The rest of the population lived in poor cottages and worked as rural laborers. Many of these cottage people also emigrated to America.

Another factor was that cities were more numerous and more evenly dispersed in Denmark than in Norway and Sweden. In Denmark, the nearest city was never more than a few hours away, even in the days of horse and buggy. In Norway and Sweden, on the other hand, it might take days to come to the nearest town.

Under these circumstances, many Danish families from the country simply went to the nearest town to seek work. Only when that failed did they consider going to America. But many people from Norway and Sweden did not try urban life in their own countries first. They emigrated directly to America. Many of them settled on farms in the Midwest.

Norwegian and Swedish emigration to America began some ten or twenty years earlier than Danish emigration. When the first mass migration of Danes began, there were already well established colonies of Norwegians and Swedes in America. These colonies served to attract new waves of immigration. Nothing was so tempting as the opportunity to come over to friends and relatives who already knew about life in America and could meet you when you arrived.

A family leaving Seljestad, Norway, in 1884.

Emigration from Scandinavia

per thousand of
population.

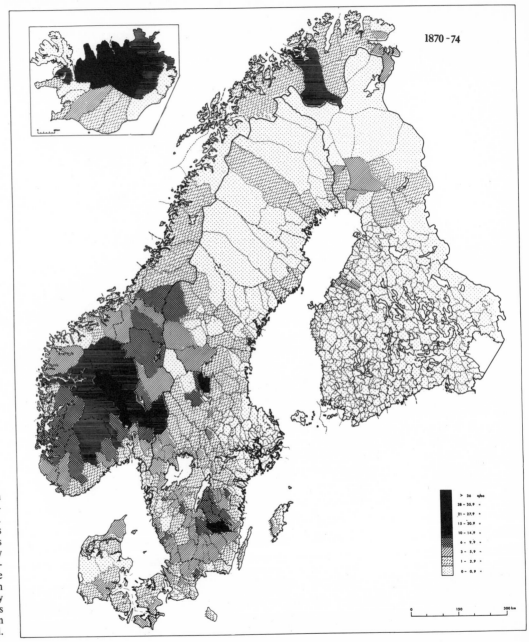

1870-74

▮	> 36 o/oo
▮	28 - 35,9 »
▦	21 - 27,9 »
▨	15 - 20,9 »
▤	10 - 14,9 »
▦	6 - 9,9 »
▨	3 - 5,9 »
▨	1 - 2,9 »
░	0 - 0,9 »

0   150   300 km

Emigration from
Scandinavia per thou-
sand of population.
The map shows
emigration in the years
1870-1874. Norway
had the most emigra-
tion as a whole. The
rate for northern
Iceland was also very
high. Emigration was
just starting from
66 Denmark and Finland.

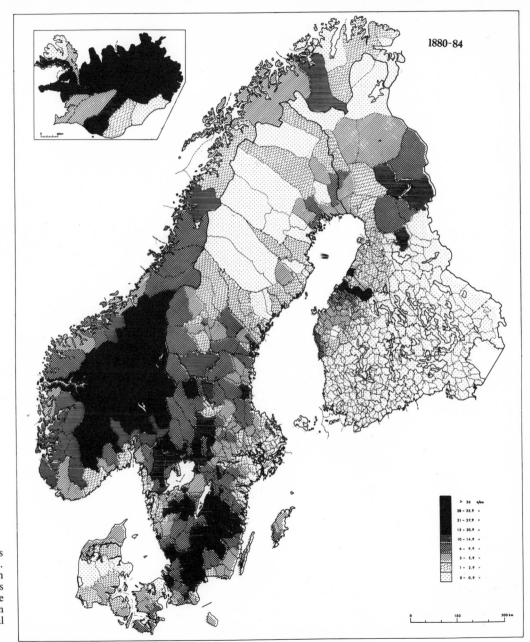

1880-84

> 36 o/oo
28 – 35,9 "
21 – 27,9 "
15 – 20,9 "
10 – 14,9 "
6 – 9,9 "
3 – 5,9 "
1 – 2,9 "
0 – 0,9 "

0   150   300 km

Emigration ten years later in 1880-1884. Norwegian emigration had reached enormous proportions. The same was true of northern Iceland and central Sweden.

67

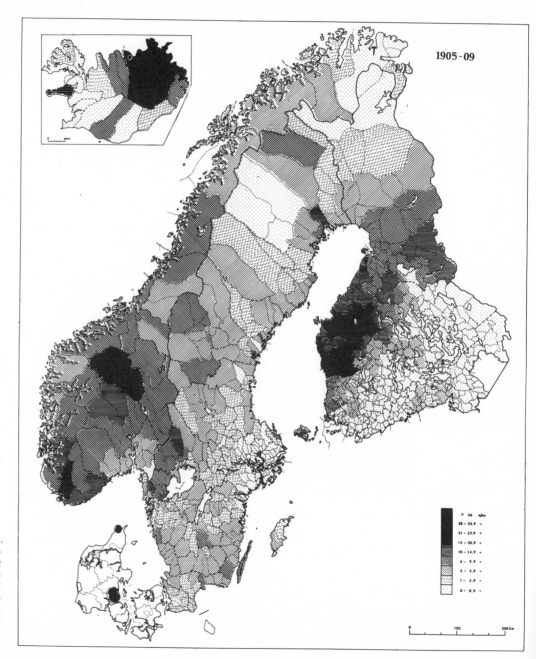

1905-09

Emigration from Scandinavia 1905-1909. The Norwegian emigration had tapered off, but that from western Finland had increased. Denmark still had less than the other countries.

68

Legend:
> 36 o/oo
28 – 35,9 "
21 – 27,9 "
15 – 20,9 "
10 – 14,9 "
6 – 9,9 "
3 – 5,9 "
1 – 2,9 "
0 – 0,9 "

0   150   300 km

America Fever

Ola from Maggebysetter

In her autobiography, the Swedish novelist, Selma Lagerlof, told about the cottagers on a farm who got together each day to eat their lunch. One day an old man, crippled by arthritis, started talking. His name was Ola from Maggebysetter.

He said, "I've had a hard and poor life. But now I've heard about a land called America, and I want to go there."

The others were lost in their own thoughts. None of them said a word. But Ola kept talking, "You see, America is like this. You just take a stick and hit the mountain, and out flows the finest brandy. I want to see that country before I die."

The others did not say a word. They all sat quietly, looking straight ahead, and they smiled.

But Ola did not give up.

"Nobody can make me stay in this country with all the toil and trouble we have, when I know there's a land where the mountains are full of fine brandy."

The others said nothing, but not a word of what Ola was saying had been wasted on them.

"And the leaves on the trees in that land are nothing but gold," said the miserable old man. "You don't have to be a day laborer on

When the immigrants wrote home, they sometimes sent postcards that used trick photography to show impossible things like these geese going to market, 1910.

an estate over there. You just go into the forest and pick yourself an armful of leaves. Then you can buy whatever you want. Yes sir, I'm going over there, old as I am.''

This put all of them into a good mood, those poor laborers on a Swedish farm. They imagined a country where brandy flowed from the mountains and where you could pick gold leaves from the trees.

Then the bell rang and lunch time was over. Out they went, into the cold and snow. But none of them had the gaunt look they had had a half hour before. There was a little glimmer in their eyes.

They all thought it was good to know about a place—even if it was so far away that they could never go there—it was still good to know that a country existed where brandy mountains tower and golden forests grow.

"The Flight to America"

Many of Selma Lagerlof's day laborers and cottagers, or their children and grandchildren, did eventually emigrate to the fabled land on the other side of the ocean.

In 1830, the Danish author, Christian Winther, wrote a book about two small boys who wanted to run away to America. This is how the older brother, Peter, described America to his little brother, Emil. The name of the book was *The Flight to America:*

America is far away,
It's twice as far as Appleby
And you must sail both night and
    day
Upon the waves, across the sea.

But when you make it over there
They give you a plantation free
And you will never have to care
For money grows on bush and
    tree.

The horses all wear silver shoes
And wagon wheels are silver too,
Gold nuggets lie around to choose
You just bend down and take
    a few.

Confection raisins, almonds grow
On bushes, both in sun and shade,
Chocolate and lemon drops fall
    like snow
The rain is pinkish lemonade.

And everyone has freedom there
In every place and every way;
Spit on the floor, no one will
    care,
Or smoke cigars the whole long
    day.

Da obned' Morun sil vandue på klem. | og råkte på vore navne.

Alfred Schmidt's illustration to Christian Winther's tale about two Danish boys who dreamed of going to America.

You sit and rock your days away
In rocking chairs, not on a stool,
And you're the only one to say
If you stay home or go to school.

America Letters

The strongest encouragement to emigration was in letters from friends and neighbors who had already gone to America. These letters often contained awkward descriptions of life in a strange land. But the style made no difference. It was the information that counted, and that was fantastic.

People in Europe could read about wages that were sky high compared to what they could earn. In some letters, they could read of friends and relatives who had big farms after only a few years of work.

Letters from America might be read by a whole village. They might even be printed in the local newspaper. Nobody doubted the facts in these letters. They had been written by people they knew and loved.

Of course, people never stopped to think that the letters only showed the good side of things. The America letters confirmed their expectations of America, and that was the important thing to them.

America letters led many people to investigate the possibility of traveling to the New World and experiencing these great adventures for themselves.

This illustration from Christian Winther's *The Flight to America* shows what expectations Peter and Emil had of the land across the ocean.

An "America Letter"

Excerpt from a letter written in 1860 by a Mormon immigrant to her family in Denmark:

"Ane Marie Mortensen, Moroni in Sanpete County, February 16, 1860. Dear unforgettable parents, sisters and brothers. I take my pen today with happiness, and I can tell you that I am very well. I arrived happy and well in Zion.

"Dear Mother, I thank you with unspeakable joy in my heart for your letter to me of March 9, 1859, which I received on February 14, 1860. I can truly tell you my situation here, and I am glad that you want to know about it. I am still a Mormon. I was married three years ago to a bachelor from England, also a Mormon, and we are happy together, serving the Lord our Heavenly Father. We have a little son who was two years old November 12, and a little girl born November 9, now a little more than three months old. The boy is named William. The girl is named Ellen Marie, which is my husband's mother's name. They are two beautiful children, and I know you would be pleased to see them.

"...We have two young steers and two young cows that will calve in April, three sheep, one lamb and we expect more, and we have six chickens and one rooster, and in a few days we are getting a pig. We have a good house and big garden—almost as big as Christian Toft's, I think.

We also have much good land, better than you have ever owned or seen in all your days. We have pasture like everyone else because it is held in common. There is so much grass that thousands of hay loads are never used. Here is the best soil ever plowed and planted. It is never fertilized, and most men harvest between five and six hundred bushels of wheat a year. We have many kinds of fruit in our garden that you would not recognize, and I live better here than I did in old Denmark. I have a deep longing in my heart to see you, dear parents, sisters and brothers, and my prayer to my Heavenly Father is that He never give you peace in your hearts until you go forth and make a covenant with your Creator and come here to this land that the Lord has promised to His people…"

Self-Sufficient in Two Years

The following is an excerpt from a letter that a Norwegian in Wisconsin sent home in September, 1845. It was printed in the Kristiansand, Norway, newspaper the following year:

"...Let us imagine that a young country lad, willing to work, who has saved up 30 or 40 dollars, leaves Norway with the idea of emigrating to America. He appears out West with a few dollars in his pocket. His goal must be to find work, and the sooner the better. This he will obtain by consulting with his fellow countrymen. He will get daily wages that vary according to the season of the year and other circumstances, from sixty cents to a dollar a day—winter sixty cents, spring eighty cents without board, and summer and harvest time, a dollar with free food. The average wage is eighty cents, of which thirty cents is spent for good food and for clothing. Thus he has saved fifty cents a day.

"If the number of work days in a year is 250, he will have saved $120 at the end of the year. Steady work earns $10 a month, often $12, and good food is included, so at that rate he will have earned $120 from which the cost of his clothing will have to be subtracted.

You can easily see that after two years, he can have saved $200 in any case. He can buy forty acres of land for $50.

"With the rest of his money, he builds his house, buys livestock, tools, etc. He can marry without worrying and, in all likelihood, look forward to a pleasant and happy future....

"If this young person had stayed in Norway, I don't think anybody will dispute the conclusion that he would be in about the same situation at the end of two years as in the beginning...

"With respect to the government, we can be nothing but pleased. Taxes and burdens do not weigh on us. For a forty acre parcel of land, you pay about a dollar a year. There is no road duty. The roads are paid for and kept up by the state. There are no poor people, so no welfare. Officials behave as you might expect in a truly free country. They are willing to serve, mild and polite to all—not the proud and repulsive manner of officials I have been subjected to in my old homeland. If a peasant in Norway has anything to do with a public official, he can usually expect to meet with a proud arrogance that witnesses to the fact that the official class see themselves as creatures of a superior order...."

It is not strange that such a letter made an impression. In a way, it is even more fantastic than the fantasies of Ola from Maggebysetter or Christian Winther's *The Flight to America*. You could become a self-sufficient person in two years if you simply worked. Could anything be more encouraging or hold out greater promise than that?

Agents

If you had money, it was just as easy to get to America as it is today to take out insurance.

To take out insurance, all you have to do is contact an insurance agent. The rest takes care of itself. That same evening, the man will probably be in your living room. He will tell you that your belongings are worth more than you think. And he will try to get you to take out two or three other insurance policies as well.

Insurance agents work this way, because they earn money for each policy they sell. The more they sell, the more they earn.

The same is true of the "America agents." They were people who sold tickets on the big passenger liners to America. There

A Children's Book About America, 1868

Five illustrations from the book, *Child Life in America,* published in Denmark in 1868. The drawings are by Lorenz Frolich. In the last picture, they are cooking maple syrup.

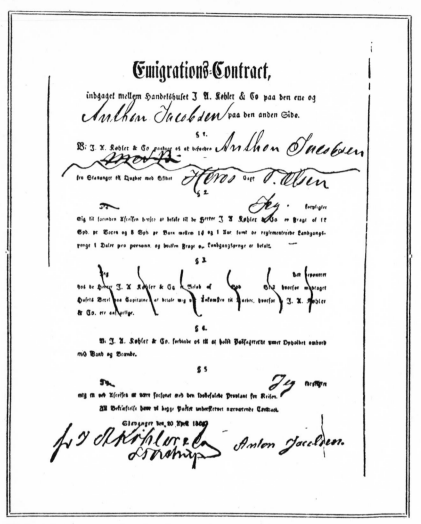

Contract for passage to America, drawn up between one Anton Jacobsen and a trading company in Norway.

Advertising Tickets

There were many kinds of ticket agents, and almost everybody had contact with them at one time or another.

Many people wrote directly to the general agents in the big cities. It was not hard to locate their names and addresses. They advertised in local newspapers. Thousands of people wrote to these agents and asked for information about ticket prices and about the country they might be coming to.

Many people wrote to several agents. They wanted to find out who sold the cheapest tickets. A ticket from northern Europe cost about $50 in 1880. That was a lot of money in those days. It was equal to several months' wages for a skilled craftsman.

But competition between passenger lines from several countries drove the price of tickets down from time to time. Meanwhile, wages were rising. By 1905, it was a good deal less expensive to sail to America by steamship, and it was a lot easier to earn the price of a ticket.

Besides the general agents in the big port cities, there were many subagents in small towns, villages and neighborhoods. They sold steamship tickets as a sideline.

were many of these agents, and they could earn quite a lot of money if they sold a lot of tickets.

The steamship companies and their agents transformed emigration to America into a big business. They may even have persuaded people to emigrate who might otherwise have stayed at home.

Competing agents swarmed around the bewildered emigrants when they arrived in the large port cities of Europe on their way to America. This satirical cartoon is from 1882.

Steamship agencies along the harbor of Copenhagen in the late 1800's.

Typical subagent's advertisement. This man had a tobacco shop and also sold tickets to America.

rest of the family could come over.

In many cases, this was the only possible way the family could afford to come to America. But the agent preferred that the whole family traveled together. Other-

American railroads also sold tickets in European countries. You could buy your steamship and railroad tickets from the same agent.

▼

They had brochures and posters advertising the voyage to America. People could look over this tempting literature themselves. It told how pleasant it was to sail in spacious ships. The brochures also told about the beautiful scenery in the New World. But the subagent did not leave everything up to the brochures. He was a good salesman. He helped people plan their trip. Maybe he knew a place where they could sell their furniture before they left. He could also tell them what they needed to take along.

Sometimes the father would emigrate first. He would work in America for a year or so. Then he would send back money, and the

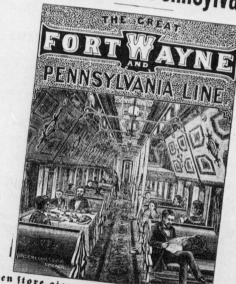

wise, he risked the chance that the husband would buy the other tickets in America and send them directly to the family back home.

Broadside Ballads

Broadside ballads were very popular a hundred years ago. They were printed sheets containing songs about love, dramatic events, or famous people. They were sold in the streets, city squares and market places. They usually cost a penny or two.

The songs were not great literature, but they were very popular. Few people could afford a newspaper or books, but almost anybody had a penny or two for a song that gave a lively impression of what people thought or what they were doing.

Broadside ballads were carefully saved. They were read and re-read many times. People learned them by heart and sang them to tunes they already knew. These ballads gave a picture of the big world outside of the little world of everyday life.

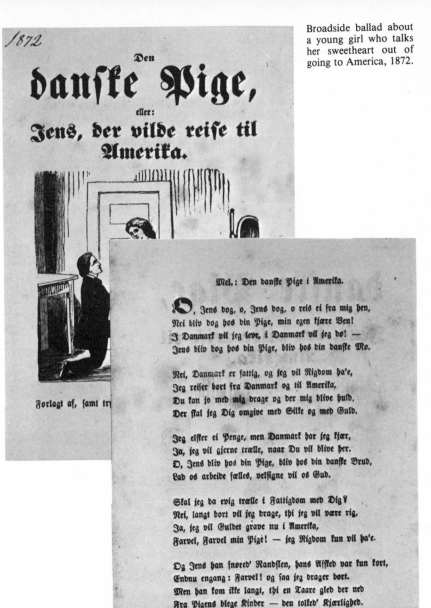

Broadside ballad about a young girl who talks her sweetheart out of going to America, 1872.

Stories about Buffalo Bill were an exciting part of the dream of America. These pamphlets are from 1904.

Den uforfærdede Buffalo Bill anbragte sig bag et mægtigt Træ, der fuldstændig dækkede ham.

Photography and Drawings

The first photographs are from the 1830's. They are called daguerreotypes after their French inventor, Daguerre. They were mostly portraits. This type of photography could not record things that moved.

The technique of photography improved rapidly. By the 1870's and 1880's, it became possible to take pictures of big events, whole sections of a city, and large groups of people.

One of the best photographers of that era was the Danish immigrant, Jacob A. Riis. He took pictures of New York immigrant neighborhoods and wrote a book called *How the Other Half Lives.* The volume, *Gateway to America: New York City,* in this series, *The Dream of America,* tells more about Jacob A. Riis and his photographs.

In those days, they had not yet discovered how to print photographs in newspapers. Drawings were used instead. The artists could make their drawings more dramatic than photographs. So a drawing and a photograph can give very different information about the same event.

Drawings of America made it seem to be a very exciting place.

Photograph of beggar children in Stockholm, Sweden, during the 1870's.

Film

Shortly after 1900, the first motion pictures were produced. Many of them told about the Wild West. They showed battles between cowboys and Indians, or between bandits and honest pioneers. At first, they were silent films. Sound movies were introduced in 1927.

Just to see people moving in pictures was fantastic. Cowboy films were very popular. They strengthened the dreams of many people about coming to the fantastic land of America.

But by the time movies were invented, the days of immigration were coming to an end.

The Last Push

Even some of the best agents lacked one thing that made it hard to convince people to emigrate to America. Often they had not been there themselves. They could show

Trangviksposten

Organ for Trangvik og Omegn

No. 3.   Udkommer hver Onsdag og Lordag i stort 2 Spaltet Format og koster 2 Kr. Halvaaret, ombragt i husene eller sendt med Posten.   20. Aarg.

Typical "Yankee," as shown in a Norwegian newspaper drawing.

Scene from a Western film.

brochures and pass on the information they had read or been told, but they could not speak with the authority of a person who had actually been there.

But the so-called "Yankees" certainly could. Yankees were emigrants who came back to visit their native country. Their tickets were paid for by the steamship line, but in return, they had to attract a certain number of emigrants.

Having a Yankee come for a visit must have been quite an experience. It was like the American Dream come to life. The prosperity and fine clothing of the Yankee was proof that you could believe what he said. He could also offer something that meant a great deal to the emigrants. He could go with them on the voyage and guide them through the many problems in the New Land.

The Yankees gave many emigrants the final push in making their big decision. Perhaps they played an important part in generating the "America fever" that dominated Europe for more than fifty years.

The Big Wave

Yankees, agents and advertisements were all links in a grand

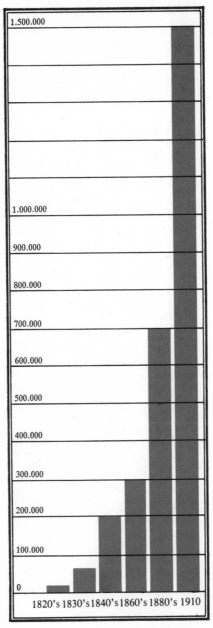

European emigration per year, 1820-1910.

system. The driving forces were the big shipping interests and the American railroad companies. You can read more about the whole system of transportation and its effect upon emigration in *The Westward Journey,* the next volume in this series on *The Dream of America.*

The emigration statistics make the large scale of the movement very clear.

During the 1820's, about 15,000 people emigrated from Europe each year. In the 1830's, about 60,000 emigrated every year. In the 1840's 200,000; in the 1860's 300,000; in the 1880's 700,000; and around 1900, one million every year.

This increase was not really an even development. There were wars and crises during some periods. Then the rate of emigration fell. But when the crisis or war was over, emigration came back even bigger than before.

Emigration reached its high point around 1910. One and a half million people were leaving Europe for America every year. Then came the First World War. Emigration had to stop during the war, and it never returned to its earlier strength. After the war, Congress passed a number of laws to control immigration. The emigrants headed for other countries instead: Canada, South America, Australia and New Zealand. But those places were not able to take as many immigrants as the USA had been able to absorb.

The fact that emigration grew so rapidly in the late 1800's and the early 1900's was obviously not due entirely to the appealing propaganda of travel agents. It was also connected with the fact that ships had become better and cheaper, and the fact that wages had increased in Europe. Every year, more and more people could afford the trip to America.

Italian immigrants arriving at Ellis Island. Immigrants had to stay there until they had been examined and questioned. If they passed the physical and mental examinations, they could enter the USA.

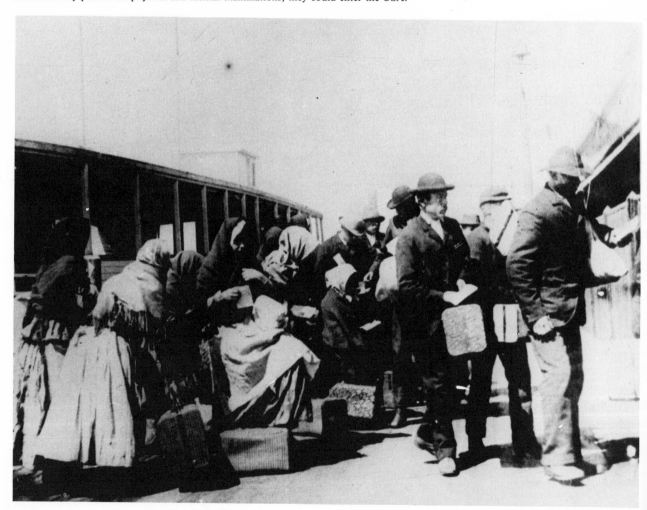

The Effects of Migration

Agriculture and Workers' Wages

What was the significance of this great mass migration? Did it have good or bad effects? The answer depends on whether it is seen from the point of view of Europe or of America.

Immigration was a disaster for the Native Americans. Otherwise, it might be said that immigration was a good thing for America in many ways. It provided people to fill the vast regions of the west and midwest. It made possible the cultivation of the prairie and the export of tremendous amounts of food to the rest of the world. Immigration got American industry going. It helped to make the USA into a world power.

Probably the beneficial effect was greatest in the beginning, when America was still thinly populated and when European immigrants settled mainly in the frontier areas of the country.

Around 1900, the more unfortunate aspects of immigration began to appear. The steady increase in the number of workers meant that wages did not have to rise. There were many workers for

The home of a Swedish immigrant, Joseph Hanson, on the South Dakota prairie in 1908.

Chinese railroad workers in the 1870's.

every job. Immigrants from Europe did not demand high wages, as long as they could earn more than they had back home. This made it very difficult for American workers to demand better pay. Wages actually went down a little in the twenty years from 1895 to 1914. The situation of workers in this period is discussed in *Shattered Dreams: Joe Hill,* in this series on *The Dream of America.*

Factory owners were happy to have immigrants who kept wages down. It allowed the owners to make more money for themselves, and also to buy more machinery and expand their factories. But the workers were dissatisfied. In the

1880's and 1890's, pressures from workers led to legislation that prohibited immigration of Chinese and Japanese, who were willing to work for low wages. After World War I, limitations were placed on immigration from all countries. Quotas were set up for each country. The number of immigrants had to be less than the yearly quota.

The quota system cut immigration in half. And the quotas kept getting lower. For example, in 1929, only 1,181 Danes were allowed to enter the USA under the quota system. That was not very many, compared to the 10,000 who had emigrated from Denmark to America in a single year before

1914.

The cutbacks on immigration were especially hard on the eastern and southern European countries. Total past immigration from these countries had not been too high because immigration from these countries had started at a late date. But total past immigration was the major factor in setting quotas. So these countries had very low quotas.

Limits on immigration did result in higher wages in America, but it also led to labor shortages. It became especially hard to find people to take the poorest paid and most unpleasant kinds of jobs. This was discovered for the first time during the First World War, when a large number of men were drafted into the armed forces.

Employers responded to the war-time labor shortage by actively recruiting Blacks in the south to come north and take the jobs. Employment agents were sent into the south to tell about the great opportunities in the industrial areas of the north. They promised better pay, better housing, and the right to vote.

Blacks in the south had bad living conditions. The Civil War had put an end to slavery, but the Blacks were still dependent upon whites. They could only get work from whites. White employers did not trust the Blacks, and they suppressed them almost as much as under slavery. Very few Blacks went to school, and even fewer had the right to vote.

Therefore, many Blacks listened to the agents. They moved north in the hope of finding a better life. In some ways, they found what they were looking for. Wages were higher and they did get the right to vote. But they had to live in slums. The immigrants moved out and they moved in.

Blacks in Harlem in New York City.

Many Blacks still live in the slums of the large American cities. Conditions have not improved as much for them as they have for others. They seem doomed to stay in the most hopeless and depressing sections of the cities.

Why is this so? Why have so many Blacks been doomed to stay in the slums while immigrants have gradually become more prosperous and moved to the suburbs? This is a perplexing problem, but a large part of the answer seems to be *racism.* Black Americans belonged to a different race than white Americans. But the immigrants did not. They were white Europeans. Therefore, they were given opportunities that were denied to the Blacks simply because of their race.

Blacks had been forced to change from an African way of life to a slave way of life, and then from a slave way of life to a free American way of life. They were denied the right to maintain their own culture. But the way of life of the immigrants was not so much different from that of white Americans. They did not have to change their culture so much in order to prosper in America.

Effects in Europe

What did emigration mean for countries like Ireland, Norway, Sweden and the other countries that gave large parts of their population to the New World?

Many believe that emigration was a good thing. It helped to ease the pressure of population growth, and it lessened unemployment. Emigration did not just help those who left. It also helped those who stayed at home. It led to a labor shortage at home. This meant that jobs were available and wages increased.

It is a fact that emigration slowed down the population growth of Europe. However, we cannot simply assume that Europeans are better off today than they would have been without emigration.

Some people argue that the total effect of emigration was harmful to Europe. They assert that many emigrants belonged to the best elements of the population of European countries.

Of course there were also exceptions. Sometimes those who could not work were given tickets to America so the European authorities would not have to support them on welfare. In some instances, criminals were sent to America instead of to jail. Finally, some families sent their "black sheep" to America. On the whole,

however, these were exceptions.

As a rule, it was not the poorest people who emigrated. The ticket to America was too expensive for them. Some people sold all of the household furnishings and still did not have enough money to buy a ticket. Here is a list of what a 48 year old carpenter owned in 1886, when he sold it all in order to emigrate:

1 sofa	$5.00
2 tables	2.00
1 bed	1.25
1 chest	1.75
4 chairs	2.00
1 mirror	.50
2 pair of clogs	.25
1 gazebo	1.25
Kitchen utensils	.65
Miscellaneous	2.75
Total	$17.40

Prices were very low in those days. But this furniture was still worth about twice as much as the carpenter got for it. That is often the case when selling used things. Still, it is hard to believe that a 48 year old craftsman did not have more material possessions than this. The sale only gave him enough money for one ticket to America. If he wanted to bring his wife and children along, he would

First Class lounge on a ship in 1904. Here it was really as nice as the advertisements showed, but it was expensive.

Third Class on the same ship. This was the way most people had to travel.

have to borrow the extra money. Otherwise, he would have to travel alone and send tickets for the others at a later time.

For those who did not earn very much and did not own anything they could sell, the voyage to America would have to remain a dream.

Mortgaging a village cooper's house. Painting by Christian Dalsgaard, 1859.

The European countries lost a great deal of money when people emigrated. It was not just the tickets that cost money. People also brought along all of their savings and earnings. Emigrants knew that they needed all the money they could scrape together in order to get off to the best possible start in the New World. In many cases, small fortunes were involved. Even if they later sent back money to relatives in Europe, it was not always as much as they had taken with them in the first place.

Labor also disappeared when the emigrants left. They were almost always in the prime of life. The European countries had paid for their growing up and their education. America was now getting them free and clear.

Emigration meant that the demand for goods declined in Europe. In many parts of Europe, this had disastrous results for the growth of industry. In other places, emigration created local shortages of labor, so people from one part of Europe migrated to another part, looking for jobs.

The Safety Valve

One of the most important results of emigration was that it probably prevented a general European revolution. It suppressed unrest in many countries and weakened the movements that were working for radical change.

The people who were most dissatisfied were also those who were most likely to emigrate. Emigration was an outlet for their dissatisfaction. In a sense, emigration was a safety valve. It let steam out of the European boiler at a time when it was about to explode.

Europe was full of dissatisfied people in the half century leading up to the First World War. Not all of them suffered from real deprivation, but they felt that they were not sharing in the technological progress they could see around them. Without the possibility to emigrate, many of them might have revolted against the oppression they felt in European society.

As was mentioned earlier, France was the only large European country that did not have a significant rate of emigration. It is probably no coincidence that France had many revolutions in the nineteenth century. In 1871, revolutionary workers seized control of the city of Paris and ruled it

Polish workers and their overseer in Denmark.

Unemployed workers in Oslo, Norway, 1888.

Paris after the defeat of the revolutionaries in 1871.

91

until they were defeated by the French army.

The Paris Revolt of 1871 had only limited effect in other countries. Almost everywhere else, emigration acted as a kind of insurance against political unrest. Those in power remained in power because their most bitter opponents emigrated to the New World.

This situation lasted until World War I broke out in 1914. This war marked an end to the period of mass emigration. In many other ways, it saw the old European world crumble and fall apart.

Italian immigrants wait for the ferry to take them from Ellis Island to Manhattan.

Index

Picture Credits

Barfoed, Janus: 82 below
Canadian Pacific: 10 above
Catlin, George: 9 above
Copenhagen City Museum: 77
Danish Labor Movement Archives: 25, 27 below
Dean; received through Matt Leskovec: 62
Denmark's Educational Library: 26 right, 75
Denver Western Library: 86
Engraving Collection, Copenhagen: 30, 31
Gothenburg Maritime Museum: 85
Gyldendal: 12 right
IFOT: 43
Illustreret Tidende: 8 left, 33
Library of Congress: 16
Lolland-Falster Diocesan Museum: 19, 91 above
Medical History Museum, Copenhagen: 20 below, 21
National Gallery, Oslo: 91 middle
Nordic Museum, Stockholm: 24
Norwegian Folk Museum: (Wilse) 58, 65, 89 (2); 76, 77 above
Oklahoma Historical Society: 13 above
Oplands-Tidende: 26 left
Politikens Pressefoto: 87
Radio Times Hulton Picture Library: 91 below
Rijksmuseum Vincent van Gogh: 23 (3), 29
Royal Library, Copenhagen: 5, 12 left, 14, 22, 35, 36, 39, 41, 45,
    46, 47, 48, 49, 51, 55, 72, 73, 78, 79, 80
Scenes by Dorse: 60
Schmidt, Alfred: 70, 71
Science Museum, London: 27
Shulman, T., The Old Country, 1974: 52, 53, 54, 56
Source unknown; received through Immigration History
    Research Center, University of Minnesota: 61, 63
Sommerville, Martin: 10 below
State Museum of Art, Copenhagen: 37, 90
Trangviksposten: 82 above
Tonnies/K. Johannesen: 32, 42
Union Pacific Railroad Museum: 11, 40
USIS: 7, 9 below, 15, 17, 18, 28, 57 above, 84, 92
Utvandrarnas Hus, Växjö: 8 right, 13 below, 69, 81
WHO: 20 above, 32